335

Heinrich Hecht

SAILING FASCINATION

Text by Hans-Harald Schack

Photos: Heinrich Hecht/www.heinrichhecht/de
Text: Hans-Harald Schack
Translated from the German by Dr. Edward Force

Originally published in Germany by Heel Verlag GmbH, Gut Pottscheidt, 2009 as Segel Faszination.
Library of Congress Control Number: 2012949409

ISBN: 978-0-7643-4268-4
Printed in Hong Kong

Published by Schiffer Publishing, Ltd.
4880 Lower Valley Road
Atglen, PA 19310
Phone: (610) 593-1777; Fax: (610) 593-2002
E-mail: Info@schifferbooks.com

In Europe, Schiffer books are distributed by
Bushwood Books
6 Marksbury Ave.
Kew Gardens
Surrey TW9 4JF England
Phone: 44 (0) 20 8392 8585; Fax: 44 (0) 20 8392 9876
E-mail: info@bushwoodbooks.co.uk
Website: www.bushwoodbooks.co.uk

HEINRICH HECHT

SAILING FASCINATION

Text by Hans-Harald Schack

Schiffer Publishing Ltd
4880 Lower Valley Road • Atglen, PA 19310

The star-class fleet at the Olympic Games in Barcelona. The German boat (left, to windward) has made a perfect start.

Contents

Making Fascination Come to Life

Jochen Schümann

Heinrich Hecht met me more than twenty years ago as press speaker for Kiel Week. The DDR team (as our squad was called in the West) was in Kiel under close public scrutiny. It was progress that East and West German sailors could not only measure up internationally at World Championships and Olympic Games, but also be neighbors over the wall. The people of Kiel were outstanding hosts, and Hecht was the man who amiably created for us the public appearance that we wanted to have. At that time others took care of protection from the press, which is very nice at times, but that we found to be disturbing.

If anyone had predicted to me in 1988 in what circumstances I would meet this friendly Kiel spokesman in the following decades, I would only have shaken my head. At our first meeting it was not clear to me that Hecht is really a photographer, but I could tell that in the years after the fall. We met at Olympic regattas and the America's Cup, which he photographed already, when I could not hope to see these boats close-up. We met at the Admiral's Cup and the MedCup, we saw each other at major events and exciting appointments. We lived with Rudi Magg on Lake Constance when Hecht photographed the Aerosail Campaign for Mercedes-Benz, my first major project in the West. He let me stay overnight with him when we presented a talk with his photos. In 1993 I picked him up from a superhighway at the Polish border where his new car had broken down. In exchange, he accompanied me just four hours later, at 5:30 A.M., to morning training at a talent scouting on the Müggelsee. At a journalists' regatta in Warnemünde, also in 1993, in which Jesper Bank also sailed, I acted as his tactician. We won, and he grinned: "That was my revenge for your defeat against Jesper at the Olympic Games in Barcelona."

A good photographer has one quality that a press speaker also needs: He can walk up to people and they look them straight in the eyes. Or in one eye, for between a photographer and his object there is usually a lens.

Heinrich Hecht sees things that can be seen only by one who knows something about the subject. The fascination that radiates from his pictures is the fascination that sailing holds for him. There are sports photographers who do not play soccer (or tennis), and yet they photograph that type of sport. They catch exciting moments, but no pictures that reflect the whole spectrum of their sport. Heinrich Hecht expends considerable effort to take his pictures and has not lost the eye for seeming trivialities. In fact, a revealing photo places sailing newcomers in the foreground while the America's Cuppers glide past behind them, a photograph with a flair for the essentials. For twenty years or longer, Hecht has photographed the most expensive yachts and most refined boats in the world, but he does not delay for a second if he sees a folkboat or dinghy in a picturesque setting.

I look forward to the next twenty years with the photos of Heinrich Hecht.

Jochen Schümann
October 2009

Jochen Schümann
Im Oktober 2009

Jochen Schümann of the German Admiral's Cup team at the helm of the Rubin XIV.

Photographing At Sea

Captains and ship owners have always wanted to have pictures of their ships. They were contracted for with artists. In the Nubian desert a 5000-year-old rock drawing of a sailor has been found; in the burial chamber of the royal agricultural recorder Menna, the ship of his pilgrimage was portrayed precisely with twelve clew-lines. When the concept of "photography" was defined by a Berlin journalist in 1839, it was still a long way to today's yacht photography. But one thing was clear: Whoever thinks he amounts to something will want to have his ship photographed from now on.

At first the new medium was naturally unsuitable for sailing photography. Ships move, even when they lie at anchor, and in the Daguerreotypes, as the first photographic process was named after its inventor, exposures had to be several minutes long. Nor could the pictures be impressively hung on the wall. But photography was modern and the technology developed remarkably fast, and brought something not to be taken for granted into the world of pictures: credibility. Since photos could not be printed at first, newspapers published steel engravings with the notation, "after a photograph." That indicated reality, and simultaneously stressed: Photos don't lie.

Man is a living being who places value on honesty, at least among other people. Newspaper reports with photos are more convincing that mere text. Naturally one can fake photos or embellish stories, but to do so one has to make an effort. In general, however, photos tell the truth. And whoever is wise insists, as a photographer, on this claim. A professional scrupulously prevents the falsification of his pictures. Nothing must be touched up in any way. Reworking is limited to what is necessary, such as the illumination of underexposed areas with strong contrast. Of course this credo has sometimes forgotten in these times of creative computer photo editing.

One can also falsify the photo by cropping, simply cutting people or ships away and thus changing the scene. But cropping, even for conservative observers, ranks among the legitimate means of photo reworking. That is because the photographer sometimes cannot take exactly what he wants in the picture. Anyone who works with a fixed lens and cannot choose his vantage point freely often takes more of the surroundings than he needs. Or he takes a format that the camera dictates to him. For the fisherman who moves alone on the horizon, he may not have a panoramic camera on hand. (Heinrich Hecht's 6 x 17 cm camera is a special camera for wide angles.)

A good photographer uses the valuable surface on which the image information is stored, digitally or chemically, as completely as possible. He can move nearer to the scene or bring it nearer with the right lens. The French multi-hull specialist Christian Février was one of the first yacht photographers to use a 50-300-millimeter zoom for high quality photos. Février's Canon objective was twice as expensive as the camera, but it soon paid for itself, for the photographer could already "cut" the picture is the viewer as he wanted to see it as a finished photo. Zoom objectives, of course, rank as not light-strong or sharp enough for impressive photography; from the beginning, they were something for the newspaper guys who went to the soccer game. There it was mainly a matter of the photographer catching the right moment. Technical picture quality is secondary.

Of course zoom lenses are second to none when it comes to rapidly changing situations when it comes to cutting image content. The art of the cut is isolating a subject, freeing it from its surroundings. The old sculptor's joke, "I take a block of marble and cut away everything superfluous," contains the golden rule of the photo cut. Concentrate on the essential. Sometimes the layout person also defines the format.

Heinrich Hecht also determines the image cut during shooting. It is all the same to him whether a ship is missing its bow, stern, or masthead if he is out to get something else. He does not take pictures with a guarantee of the object's completeness, but of what he sees... The photo on page 69 actually shows a crew who is looking for the finish line. If Hecht had gone higher in the helicopter, [p. 10] or had zoomed farther away, we would not see the crew in their strange, but so typical for sailing, situation, but rather the boat. Many pictures in this book were taken by the photographer at just the right position. One cannot learn that; it happens or it does not.

The star-class silver medal winner of 1984, Achim Griese, in the Dragon championship off Neustadt.

A rule for the yacht photographer is: Right to the subject. Usually he does not have enough time to think about what the subject is. Sailing is sport, and the pictures are not posed. Everything goes fast. A photographer must see the pictures, anticipate pictures, think in pictures. Otherwise he cannot photograph them. A non-photographer can be sent to the hot spots of sailing with perfect equipment, and he will at best bring back pretty pictures, but not good ones.

Yacht photographers spare no efforts to get to the subject. They charter boats and helicopters, they go to watchtowers and capes. If they go along on an organizer's photo boat, they get acceptable pictures, but the two or three others on board also have these pictures. The error of going on a big boat with a hundred scribbling colleagues is made only once by a photographer. One is at the mercy of the press boat's captain, and usually far away from a shot.

Since the hunt for the best pictures is not cheap, a yacht photographer must also be a good marketing man. There is competition, and he cannot sell photos when he has already taken them. No magazine editor plans a series of pictures from an actual regatta if he does not have a firm agreement with a photographer. Good photographers sell pictures before they exist. Unless there is some basis for a contract, an commercially minded professional does not take the trip.

Meanwhile the press agencies also deliver outstanding pictures, but they have one disadvantage for magazines: They are—except for large events—only a few photos, and every reader already knows them from the newspapers. So good yacht photographers have their buyers because they deliver more, and in general also of better quality, than an agency. But the market has become narrow.

For photographers, it is always important to be at the right place at the right time. Erich Kästner wrote in "The Flying Classroom" that he, as a writer, can describe a snowball fight even in the summer. A writing journalist can gather the facts by telephone and ask the eyewitnesses after an event is over. But the photographer is an eyewitness. He must be there. And a good photographer knows in advance where he must position himself. Naturally, he sometimes needs a bit of luck, as Hecht had with Dennis Conner. In Fremantle in 1987 Hecht, the beginner, if one remembers correctly, missed the time of the victory celebration. But then he had the good luck to get a better shot of Conner from his late position than all those experienced competitors. Luck? Of course. But one should not overlook that Hecht had helped luck along a bit by marching five kilometers along the other side of the harbor with his heavy equipment, climbing over an armada of spectators' rubber boats and catching Conner at the right second when he turned the right way when called.

A good yacht photographer goes to work prepared. He knows the weather report. He knows which way the wind will blow and when the sun will shine on the boats from what angle. Maybe he does not know it consciously, but intuitively. However, he knows whether he will get a chance, on what course he'll see the crew's faces, where maneuvers will be made, whether he must take pictures against the wind and spray. If he sees the deck of a ship from the lee, the crew is hidden on the high angle behind the sail. If he is moving behind a ship sailing into the wind, he can get a good shot of what is happening in the cockpit—and of the backs of the crew's heads as they all look tensely at the spinnaker. One has to be moving ahead of the ship to be sure one is moving faster than the photographed yacht, otherwise there will be very angry words, and at worst, a wreck.

Editors-in-chief and photo editors are the most critical observers of photos, and for the yacht photographer in the truest sense of the word, the decisive ones. They want to know what is to be seen in the picture, and are at first blind to the beauty of a subject. Sometimes, of course, they choose a picture only for its beauty. Yet they want to know first what they see.

A photographer is thus always the transporter of information. Of course there is any plenty of subjects in the yacht photographer's territory that do not require any further information, and that one can print "without words," such as posters, wallpaper, calendars, or other photographic images.

Yachts are expensive. Anyone who can spend a million for a ship usually has the money to spare to hire a photographer for a day. Yet that does not happen often, for the job of a ship's portraitist has been made rare by modern photography. The owners of beautiful ships prefer to buy copies of an especially nice photo, or the copyright to it. But shipyards and boat dealers are naturally interested in having good pictures for advertising, and it is up to the sail or yacht photographer to produce them. The normal commercial photographer ashore, who photographs models or soup plates, is not suitable of photographing boats. A yacht photographer is also a design photographer. He must have a sense of line and proportion and be able to set a ship in a scene that makes it look even better, if possible, than reality.

When photographing, many are sure that it is relatively simple to take usable photos of many ships coming toward him in a regatta field. But how hard it is to photograph a single ship from a point on land so that everything is just right! It is necessary to keep in contact by cell phone or two-way radio with the ship to be photographed, the sailing "model." And it is also helpful to have spoken with the skipper in advance concerning which way he is going to sail and from which direction toward the photographer's viewpoint. The photographer gives the commands. It is naturally simpler and more professional if the photographer himself goes onto the water and can see his subject from every viewpoint. And if he gets into a helicopter, the third dimension opens to him.

Photographers are often esthetes and have the habit of photographing the world beautifully, even the decadence and collapse. Sail photographers have it easier from the start. Their world is already beautiful. Ships come into being in the course of an intensive, usually successful design process, the people on board are healthy and cheerful. That can be photographed without trouble. But it is also the art of a good sail photographer to make a beautiful picture of a tired, frozen regatta crew that drives their ship over a white foaming sea in the pale light of dawn—a picture that is true.

A yacht photographer should love sailing.

SAIL

What Moves Us

Sails are the original driving power of ships. They allow long trips for which muscle power is not sufficient. The (almost) ever-present source of energy is the wind. The bigger the sails and the tackle became, the more energy could be used, and the bigger ships could be powered. The internal combustion engine has practically replaced the sail in professional shipping by now, but the fascination with traveling by wind power remains. For us, sailing is an athletic sport, and it is also the esthetics of technique that raises sailing above experiencing nature and measuring sporting power.

Whoever sees a modern ship sees a product of aerodynamic knowledge. From the woven blanket or fur coat that one of our paddling ancestors spread out before a tail wind to the laminated present-day 3-D profiles that consist of glued foils and fibers has come a long way. The belly of a sail is—except perhaps for the spinnaker—not a belly any more, and has not been for a long time; but, instead is a defined surface that, when air flows across it from the right angle, generates propulsion in the same way the wings of an airplane creates lift. The more power a sail creates, the stronger the vessel's components must be made, as the forces generated are transmitted to the boat's structure. The sails should also be more resilient and increasingly, by the same standard, weigh less and less.

For centuries the development of better sails has been an endless experiment. Present-day regatta sails are calculated by computers and cut according to computers. Naturally, the burdens that are directed into the surface of the sail via clew, head, and neck are calculated by a computer and the number and direction of the power-transferring fibers are determined by a computer. But it is not all science and technology. The struggle with the material is human's work and thus full of surprises.

Below: Dragons off Saint-Tropez.

Right page: In the Audi MedCup off Mallorca, two TP 52s hurry along to the lee under their asymmetrical spinnakers.

MEDCUP
2
24

In the photos that Heinrich Hecht has chosen for this chapter one can sometimes ask: Where is the man here? Hecht has chosen a simple spinnaker for the cover of this book, although he has countless photos from the same regatta in which ships sail through sun-sparkling water under full sail. Hecht has—intuitively—chosen one picture that shows an individual's struggle with the hard-to-tame cloth. (Spinnakers are still sewn of woven cloth today.)

The pictures on page 22 show the technological progress made in fifty years. At right is the rig of a spread-gaff ketch, all sails cut precisely to the millimeter from cloth and sewn. One sees folds, the leech of the mizzen is supported more badly than well by the sail battens. At the left is the sail of the catamaran with which Dennis Conner defended the America's Cup against the gigantic mono of New Zealander Michael Fay. It is not a sail in the traditional sense any more, but rather a filigreed rigid wing, on which builder Burt Rutan cooperated, he who later designed the spacecraft *Space Ship One* and the *Global Flyer* with which Steve Fossett flew nonstop around the world.

Sailors love their sails. They are the wardrobe of the yacht, and "a new set of sails" is not always technically needed. The psychological effect of the expensive cloth on a regatta crew, though, is tremendous. And at the highest level of sailing sport, the new sails are often decisive in determining who crosses the finish line half a second sooner.

This rescue maneuver in Act 12 of America's Cup '07 went completely awry. The spinnaker of the Italian team's Mascalzone Latinö *drags in the wake.*
The Team Emirates New Zealand *(left page), on the other hand, has its spinnaker under control and will pull it onto the deck in a few seconds.*

"I thought I knew which sail profile was the right one, and I thought all sails should look that way. I needed four or five years to realize that I didn't have the slightest idea about sail profiles."

Lowell North, founder of North Sails, about the beginning of his business.

Like a swarm of dragonflies, the 49ers go their way with their foil sails off Kiel. The best-known name for the transparent polyester is "Mylar."

On the 75th birthday of the dragon class in 2004, 254 boats started the jubilee regatta off Saint-Tropez. There was enough room on the water, but it was cramped in the harbor.

Left: Admiral's Cup yachts in the downwind course on the Solent. There are plenty of wind and waves; the crews ride out.

Right: The wind spotter on the topmost crosstree of the TP 52, its big sail still standing perfectly, warns of calm areas and seeks wind fields.

Left: After the lee mark the Genua sail has curved into a flat profile within seconds, while the team on deck obviously is having a hard time gathering the spinnaker fast enough.

Below, left to right: Foresail, jib, and flying jib over the clipper stem are, like a single sail, easy to handle by a small crew but clearly give less thrust than one big sail.—Modern sails are complex structures of foil and special power-conducting fibers. They are cumbersome and have nothing more to do with what landlubbers mean by "cloth."—A crowd in the Maxi championship, but the spinnakers still catch enough wind. For the 25 men on board such a ship, there is plenty of work.

Left: The rigid wing of Stars & Stripes *is the most revolutionary sail that was ever used in the America's Cup. The traveling sails of the spread-gaff ketch* Senta, *sewn of especially thin strips in the traditional style, seem to come from another world.*

Right: On the water, Stars & Stripes *was a David that easily beat the* New Zealand *Goliath. When the rigid wing was first used, every detail functioned from the start. At night the unit was brought on shore and put aside, so it offered no surface for the wind to catch.*

After 1988 the America's Cup was reorganized. America3 *was one of the first IACC yachts that replaced the technically obsolete 12-meter yachts. The new class carried around 320 square meters of sail, almost twice as much as the last twelves.*

The 1988 America's Cup was seen as a mismatch, an unjust race. New Zealand *had 600 square meters of sail in the wind— and lost to Conner's little stiff-winged catamaran.*

Right: Genoa high, spinnaker away. The bow man introduced the lee maneuver.—BMW, the car maker, has been involved on the water for many years. The high-tech company profits from the image of clean high-tech sport sailing. The gigantic spinnaker of a TP 52 is cut relatively flat and still pulls on a half-wind course.

The Genoa as a projection surface. The foreshipman on BMW Oracle *prepares for the spinnaker maneuver. Spinnaker fall, clew, and afterguy are already attached.*

SPEED

Only Fast is Good

Right: Hasso Plattner's Morning Glory *while training for Cape Town. The slim high-sea racer offers a splendid view from a helicopter's perspective at full speed (below). Photographing yachts with the wide-angle lens twists the lines of a ship for everyday viewing—unless one gets into a rubber boat and takes the horizon into the middle of the picture.*

Every sailor praises his boat's top speed, which is usually reached at wind strength 8 on a downwind course when the waves help push and one can still carry quite a lot of sail. If a ship is not able to go fast, then one can at least praise its qualities in a dead calm. Joseph Conrad mentions in one of his stories ("Christening") a ship that still travels as long as the wind is sufficient to move a down feather. For seamen under sail, speed is the highest quality. In the America's Cup it was true for a long time that one needed a strong-wind ship to be fast in the elimination races and a light-wind ship to have a chance in the Cup finale.

The sail area that a ship can carry is a decisive factor for speed. Big ships can carry more sail that smaller ones; wide ships have a greater righting moment that narrow ones. For relatively small-displacement ships like yachts there is also a sort of individual sound barrier, to so-called hull speed. The old sailors' saying, "length runs," that refers to the hull speed, no longer applies today without reservation, since yachts have also learned to surf and cover long stretches in a gliding motion.

Gliding was long reserved for dinghies and surfboards. A typical yacht—and any other ship that displaces water—produces waves. At best, there are only two, namely the bow and stern wave. In between lies the wave trough. The sailing power of a normal yacht is not sufficient to push the ship over this wave.

The ship is a prisoner of its own wave system. Since large waves run through the water faster than smaller ones, the yacht with the longer water line is underway with a faster wave system at hull speed. Modern racing yachts, though, are designed so that they can leave their stern wave behind them. With enough wind they turn into big surfboards and rush over the water like motorboats. Big, fast racing yachts under ideal conditions can cover more than 600 miles in 24 hours nowadays.

In the medium of photography, it is difficult to decrease speed. A photo, after all, does not move. The blur of water rushing by can convey a sense of speed. Flying water "frozen" by the camera reproduces an event that is much too fast for the human eye. The position of the boat in the wave, the tense position of the sailor on board, are the strongest evidence of the speed of the moving boat. In order to interpret a "quick picture" correctly, one should know firsthand what it is like on the water.

The fact that the camera freezes the moment naturally adds a fascination to sail photography. The camera shows us what we are experiencing, but generally cannot really see. There is also a requirement that the photographer chooses the right moments from the wealth of material.

Gleaming sun, the water splashes past—speed in a wide-angle view. Photo editors are happy when the photographer is up close, for that gives the most dynamic pictures.

Compact power shot through to telephoto lenses. The deck in the water up to the rail, a mighty bow and stern wave. Hull speed on a downwind course.

"What joy! We never had less than 35 knots of wind. It was a hell of a ride!"

Bernhard Stamm about his 2001 Atlantic record

Dragons after the start of the Jubilee Regatta off Saint-Tropez. The first row got off well (left page). It can scarcely be imagined that it could go even faster. But the crew will now hoist the spinnaker, the boom is already in place (left). How fast the America's Cuppers move through the water despite the weak wind can be seen by the wakes of the motorboats that are underway at the same speed.

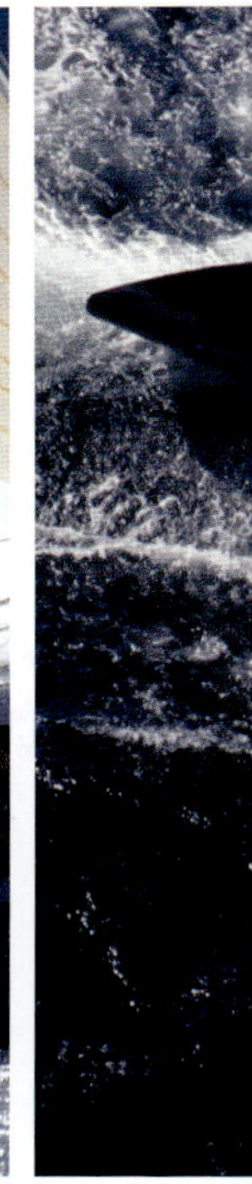

"For us it is always more exciting to take part in a new class, because in an existing class you can sense only the smallest improvements."

Alinghi *Chief Designer Rolf Vrolijk*

The camera sees more than the eye. When the bow pockets the wave impact, that comprises just a fleeting moment for the crew. The feeling of speed is real through the pressure exerted on the sheets, and the spray that regularly soaks the crew on the high angle. On big ships too, the ambitious crew trims—nothing is wasted.

FANCOURT'S Morning Glory

Platoon *on the wind with Jochen Schümann at the rudder. On the cross the whole crew functions as windward ballast. The TP 52 has a slim waterline with this heeling and runs at optimal speed.*

A rushing ride in the mistral off Marseilles. Hecht would gladly have taken more pictures, but the gusts were too unpredictable for the helicopter pilot.

CLASSIC

Beauty Lives Longest

Original accessories like this winch add a magical touch to restoring an old yacht. For these fittings were the optimal technology of their day. Yet vast quantities of modern technology are also put to use on many classic yachts. In the Prado Challenge for Classic Yachts (right) the maritime beauties meet for a week of regatta sailing off Sardinia.

Ships are not beautiful because they are old. The fact that we consider old ships beautiful today stems from two main reasons.

Old ships, so-called classics, often owe their existence today only to the fact that they are beautiful. Why should anyone go to the trouble of paying money to maintain an ugly ship beyond its natural life span? Ships that are worn out can only have new life breathed into them when there is beauty in them. They are not always yachts; they could very well be freighters, for fast, strong, capable ships have been designed especially for everyday use. There are designers who could not draw an ugly ship. William Fife, Colin Archer, von Oertzen . . . to name only a few.

Most stories of restored ships now begin: A man with money or idealism—a combination of the two is best—discovers an old ship somewhere, rotting away, that was a beauty. He decides to awaken the ship to a second life. Whether the American millionairess Elizabeth Myers saves a J-class yacht from the breakers, or a teacher rescues an old Abeking & Rasmussen cruiser, does not matter a bit.

The other convincing reason is that good ships are almost always beautiful. It is like with physics formulas. A true formula is usually elegant. The designers of past centuries thus preferred to design optically harmonious pictures. It is not true that they could not reckon—they could do it. They also knew the factors that made a ship fast or slow.

D3

There are countless examples of yachts with which a handicap formula was supposed to be tricked. But these ships are not around any more. The best regattas have for years been sailed by seaworthy yachts.

The evolution of yachts functions according to laws that follow those of nature. Antelopes further the development of leopards, and the leopards have thus made antelopes faster. Smugglers' schooners should sail faster than revenue cutters, blockade runners faster than blockaders, fishing boats should not only maintain themselves on the sea but also bring their catch to market quickly. Ships that were the best in everyday life also took part in regattas.

In Germany, Scandinavia, England, France, and the American East Coast there are now impressive "oldtimer" fleets, English "vintage yachts," or simply "wooden boats." And these fleets are growing. There are copies and restoration projects that are much more expensive than a comparable modern ship.

The photographer and the writer of this book met some years ago in Saint-Tropez. Both had traveled almost 2000 kilometers because of the classic yachts that had come there for the legendary "Nioulargue" hard regattas. It is just one of those classic ship meets, but the most famous one. And some 250 wondrous yachts gather there as a sort of floating yacht museum. With that meet we had chosen the most beautiful form of the boat show: a regatta series in which there is really hard sailing and the ships show that they are not only beautiful but also very lively.

Aschanti IV *has all sails, including its topsail, set and sails into the bay of Saint-Tropez. Most of the other yachts stayed in the harbor on that stormy regatta day in 2008.*

Schooners and gaff cutters at the start of the Regatta Les Voiles de Saint-Tropez. The ships sail by a compensation formula, but the most important thing is still to cross the finish line as the first ship home.

"Sir, you have challenged me to win this race, and by God, I'll do it."

Charlie Barr, 1905, to Wilson Marshall, owner of the three-masted schooner Atlantic *before he locked him and all the guests in the salon. Marshall had asked Barr to turn back in a storm.*

Hard work on the tilting teak deck of the Mariquita, *a William Fife yacht of 1911. There is no wall, just a rail. The sails of modern fabric are sewn in the style of the old Mako sails (above). – With no wind, life on deck is more restful. The thickness of the sheet hints at what powers move the* Orion *in a wind.*

The Marconi gaff cutter Moonbeam IV *pursues* Tuiga, *the flagship of the Yacht Club de Monaco, which is sailed by club members and is never missing from any important regatta.*

Challenge 12, *one of Alan Bond's five twelvers, a Ben Lexcen design of 1983. A sister ship beat the Americans that year after they had held the America's Cup for 132 years.*

Altair in harbor, with the afterdeck, full of people by day, empty. The regatta crew is resting in a hotel, and evening guests come in club shirts and blazers. Whoever goes on board swaps his street shoes for deck shoes. The non-skid teak deck that guarantees safe standing at sea can stand neither stones in profile soles nor penny heels. – Right: The last 19-meter yacht from Glasgow, *Mariquita*.

Les Voiles de Saint-Tropez—this is perhaps Europe's most beautiful regatta series. Classic racing yachts from more than a hundred years meet early in October to take part in competition every morning. Saint-Tropez becomes a living yacht museum.

Left: Solvay Maid *off Saint-Tropez.*

William Fife III built this fast cruising yacht at first on his own hook. She is a composite of steel ribs, a teak and oak keel, planked with mahogany.—Modern rescue rings are at hand everywhere. – Orion *under sail. Even at the rail you can see your reflection in the paint.*

K4

K7

6700 square meters in the wind, 160 tons of weight— the gigantic J-class yachts dominated the America's cup scene before the affordable twelvers took their place. The "J" stands for a waterline length between 75 and 87 feet. Cambria *(left) and* Velsheda *have been restored for more than ten million dollars each. – The 80-year-old three-masted schooner* Creole *of Alessandra and Andrea Gucci is welcome at any classic regatta week, but now and then it must anchor outside the harbor due to space limitations.*

The German twelvers Tea *and* Trivia *off the old Olympic Harbor of Kiel (left). – When* Trivia *was built by Camper & Nicholson in 1937, she was the fastest of her class. In 2007 she won ten of eighteen jubilee regattas on the hundredth anniversary of the formula. – The former Navy twelver* Ostwind *now sails under its old name of* Sphinx *again (near right). – Classic match race of the twelvers off Kiel:* Trivia *is behind* Tea *but has gained the windward position.*

12
G 4

FLY
PICTURES

The mighty lever of the boom of Moonbeam IV *requires a lot of rudder pressure (left page). — Rendezvous before the picturesque scene of Saint-Tropez: The classic yacht, the speedboat, the motor catamaran and the photographer's helicopter (lower left). –* Altair *is one of the last big yachts by William Fife III (center). –* Ranger *is a copy of the America's Cup defender of 1937 (against the British* Endeavour II*). That is when the era of J-class yachts fighting for the "can" ended.*

Owl (launched 1903) was cut apart by its owner in the twenties and lengthened eight meters. The operation succeeded; the gaff ketch sails fast.

Wayward *was built in Bristol in 1898 and was later called* Sampshire*. A hundred years after its launch, the gaff yawl was restored. (The mizzenmast is outside the water line.)*

"These yachts are the dream of every sailor. Many modern yachts, of course, are bigger but cannot equal a twelver esthetically."

Oliver Berking, organizer of the "12m World Cup."

Thendara *was in the hands of the British Army in World War II, serving as a mooring boat for moored balloons that opposed low-flying planes. Afterward it was time for a restoration. The owner, Sir Arthur Leslie Young, died in 1950, his heirs sold the ship to pay for his burial. In a general overhaul, fifty years later the high-masted ship again was given its original gaff rig.*

Still Life *in the harbor: The end of the boom is decorated by a mighty forged fitting, the wooden blocks of the sheet must take enormous pressures. A patent collar is to be avoided under all conditions.*

Moonbeam IV *on the way to the start; the crew is relaxed. Afterward, the powerful rig will require fast work on sheets and backstays.*

Altair was ordered as a "robust cruiser yacht that can sail everywhere in the greatest possible safety." Designer William Fife III also succeeded in creating a fast, elegant ship.

The gaff cutter Moonbeam IV *shortly after the collar with half a wind. The lee backstay is lowered far enough that the crew now has its hands full.*

Foresail on deck, check rope in the main sheet. The crew keeps watch for the goal line. Heinrich Hecht has focused on the man with the spyglass and the crew.

DINGHIES

AND SMALL KEELBOATS

The Fundamentals of Yachting Sport

A boat sails calmly along the shore. The national flag at the stern shows that it is not sailing in a regatta, but is just underway on a trip. The smallest long-keel boat is a perfect design. The keelboat Streamline *has existed only for a few years; it was known as a match-racing boat. Heinrich Hecht shot it in 1/8 of a second.*

Certain individuals may learn sailing on a big yacht, perhaps because they sailed with their parents as children or because friends invited them. Most people, though, begin with a small boat. The renowned Opti is by no means the ideal boat, because a child sits alone on board and is left to himself or on call from a trainer (usually his father). Two-man boats are best. Two men are already a team, they complete each other, share tasks, and perhaps also responsibility. There is a hierarchy that generally disappears behind friendship or team spirit. The foresheet man is just as important for success as the helmsman, and he has to work harder physically.

A modern dinghy requires bodily control; the boat is a sport article. Small keelboats are yachts with dinghy personality. They are already genuine "ships" with plenty of lead or steel under the keel, they right themselves if they are laid on their beam ends in a wind. And despite that, they must be sailed with full physical faculties. Almost all top sailors on big yachts have developed their abilities on the dinghy. Germany's only America's Cup winner, Jochen Schümann, for example, comes from Finland, as do most other Cup aces. The dinghy is the foundation of the yachting sport. Ted Heath, once British Prime Minister and Admiral's Cup winner, told a reporter: "Whoever has not sailed a dinghy has not learned sailing from the ground up."

Dinghies and small keelboats are democratic vehicles. Everyone can afford them, if he really wants to, in many classes even at the top level.

The robust Folkeboat is the "Volkswagen" of the keel yachts. For decades it was the most modest (and sporting) among the small seaworthy ships—no exclusive "yacht" like the Dragon.

Women, who are rarely crew chiefs on big ships, are well established on small boats. There are countless mixed and all-women crews. That is the nature of the thing: For a couple, the dinghy is the ideal shared sporting equipment, for girl friends too. Whoever makes it to the victor's podium at a big dinghy regatta must be a really good sailor, for against fifty or a hundred competitors one only wins when everything goes right. At Kiel Week, the competitors in the Olympic class are more numerous than in the Olympic Games, and just as qualified.

Photographically, dinghies are a challenge. A 470 is a completely unspectacular boat, especially when one has seen them a thousand times already. The Kiel Firth is not an exotic scene either. When Hecht awakens dinghies to life with his camera, then he shows the dynamic of the swarm, the struggle of many different talents with (almost) equal material. He shows the athletics of the small boats, in which a man is not only helmsman but also active ballast, and the closeness of the sailor to the water. The smaller the ship, the greater is nature.

At the games in Sydney, the Soling, the fastest and yet the most stable keelboat designed in 1967, sailed in its last Olympics. The Americans went without a medal, and the 1996 gold medalist, Jochen Schümann, had to be content with silver in the match race.

USA
USA

"Whoever has not sailed a dinghy has not learned sailing."

Ted Heath (British Prime Minister and Admiral's Cup winner)

The moths are among the most artistic sailboats or devices (left). The dragon, on the other hand, is a classic whose bow line incorporates a hundred years of yachting tradition. Long overhangs decrease the moistened surface of a displacement boat and improve the joy of turning.

A 420 at the Kiel Week. It is the youth entry boat for generations of ambitious dinghy sailors (left). The Streamline *crew in a perfect trapeze position. The hand behind the head relaxes the neck and lengthens the center of gravity outward (right).*

"It gives great pleasure, and I learn more every day. The smaller the ships become, the better the sailing is."

Maxi owner Hasso Plattner after his comeback in the fifties.

Independent sailing begins for the optimistic youngsters (left). Dragons on the Mediterranean off Saint-Tropez.

Classic H-dinghies—one among them is gaff-rigged (G 185) – on the Steinhuder Meer. Heinrich Hecht has sailed and maintained his own mahogany-planked H-dinghy ("my Stradivarius") for 25 years. To be able to photograph it, he occasionally lends it to his sail supplier, the Beilken business manager Jörg Müller-Arnicke, shown at the tiller here.

A 470 field at the Kiel Week. In 1988 the 470 became an Olympic women's boat. The red square on the point means that this is a women's competition. In Germany some 40 female crews sail ir the rank list.

Yves Loday and Nicolas Henard on the way to Olympic gold. In a squall they came within inches of Hecht's photo boat. Hecht told them only years later that it was he who had almost cost them the medal.

USA
GMX

America's Cuppers with a crowd of little guys. Heinrich Hecht photographed the Opti fleet at the German Sailing Grand Prix off Kiel (left page)—Flying Dutchmen with a shore wind and enormous waves at Barcelona, dragon field off Saint-Tropez, and P-boats in the 2005 Deipen Cup. As soon as they're on a headwind course and the crews hoist the spinnakers, every regatta becomes a blaze of color.

"470 men crews sail more aggressively than women. It is difficult to sail with them. We fought with two Greek boys several times, although we were, in principle, not competitors."

Geeske Genrich

The crew hangs in simple belts, the 90-year-old star-boat design is very simple in principle—three planks, a mirror, and a keel. But the old timer, which has been an Olympic class since 1932 (with a pause from 1972 to 1976), has developed into a high-tech boat and has lured elite sailors since then.

Eva Kirchner at the tiller, Bianca Niemann in the trapeze. The 470 is the boat in which ambitious women find the greatest competition worldwide. In a wind the usually heavier male crews have an advantage; thus there have been women's competitions since 1934 — 75 years of dragons! For the jubilee regatta 2004 off Saint-Tropez, Klaus Körting, Hajo Fritze, and Jürgen Plambeck traveled to the Mediterranean. Körting is five years younger than the class.

Europes before Kiel. The class was still called "Europe Moth" in the sixties because it developed from Moths. The light (132 pound [60 kilo]) boat was used in the Olympics from 1992 to 2004.

14-footers are skiffs with huge expanses of sail. Except for the length, there are no design limits. They are the fastest 14-foot class, but hard to sail.

Left: Olympics 1992, the Israeli FD crew. Right: A boat for two artists, a 14-footer off Travemünde.
Right page: In the 1993 star-class World Championship off Strande, it was essential in handling the typically short Baltic waves well. Because of the large sail area, the narrow keel-boats usually sail with a strong heel. The righting moment increases the sail pressure off to the lee.

RMW

Left page: Much wind and many waves in the sound off Newport, Rhode Island. Since the flexible mast of the dinghy is not meeting, the foresail is also more of a head-wind sail.

—This page left: F-18 catamarans off Kiel. The most popular development in this class are the Hobie Tigers, but new types are constantly being designed for this 18-foot formula.

—The mast of the star class is far forward, the mainsail with its 67.25 square feet [20.5 square meters] has almost three times as much area as the foresail. There is no spinnaker. Keeping the over-tacked boat in the wind is an art and requires strength.

—Dragons are built of wood, now as before. The open keelboats with their defined cabins look like elegant little yachts.

CREW

Able Under All Conditions

The crew is the heart and brain of a ship, it makes a slow ship fast and cannot be replaced by anything automatic. There are small family crews that seek recreation, and big regatta crews that go on the water as fighters, specialists, tacticians. The crew trims and dominates the ship. Usually though not always, there is a chief on board. Regatta crews are composed of team players who can fit in.

The owners of big ships are chiefs. Among their most important tasks is assembling a good crew. Many crews find each other more or less on their own, and they always have successors. If one cannot sail at Helgoland in May because he has to do something about his studies, or the boss won't give him time off, then someone else who fits into the team is called in. The sailing scene is a net of small networks.

When SAP founder Hasso Plattner sent his *Morning Glory* to the Capetown-Rio race, the organization had functioned wonderfully in the field; only a hotel was not booked. Regatta crews live on the sea without complaining under conditions that violate animal cruelty laws, but on land they live in hotels. Capetown was booked solid because of the many other crews, but the manager of a golf course that Plattner belongs to remembered at the right time, thanks be, that Plattner still had an empty villa in the area, known as The Embassy. The crew trained hard on board for two weeks before the race and, as Heinrich Hecht remembers, lived in the evenings like gods in France.

On big ships there are enormous powers at work, and when a backstay is released half a second too soon, it sometimes costs a mast. A wrong handgrip can have fatal results. There is enough pressure on the sheets to strike a man dead. To sail successfully, the regatta crew must find a perfect boat, whether it is for a race or for training on board. For the core crew, this means that they have the ship in order down to the slightest detail, and must master all of the technology on board.

Left: "Men at work." The muscle-men on BMW Oracle *crank power to their coffee grinders on the sheets. Whoever does not grab it soon enough hurts his fingers. Dennis Conner was the first soccer player to crank the grinder, as they are accustomed to power while lacking oxygen and hold out longer in turning duels. Today, crews complete sophisticated power and speed training (left side). Right: The foreshipman at the spinnaker sheets will pick the boom. From the bow to the cockpit, all maneuvering stations are assigned. In a good crew, each one masters several functions. With high winds, life jackets are mandatory, at least at night and in cold waters. – Following double pages, 96-97: On* Tuiga *there is even room for a little flirting on the high angle. The woman has already become aware of the photographer.*

Besides the "boat captain," who usually plays the role of a boatman at a regatta, there are a number of specialists on board, who are all-arounders, but know certain things especially well. Bowman, pitman, tactician, navigator, grinder, foreshipman. "I make the foreship" means that Pete, who could just as well explain falls and store sails below decks, makes himself so familiar with the whole foreship technology that he can get a hand on the chaos, even if the spinnaker has wrapped itself around the forestay in a dark, stormy night. And quickly at that, for the next spinnaker must be hoisted.

A crew must function. The bigger the ship, the more important the communication among the crew members is. Training on regatta yachts means that handgrips that everyone knows in principle must function smoothly, misunderstandings must be ruled out, work processes must be attuned to each other.

A crew is the soul of the ship. It resists sunburn and coldness, it overpowers mistakes and learns from them, it fights and works to total exhaustion. The names of the "men before the mast" do not usually appear in the lists of results, but the owners and helmsmen know that they could do nothing without a crew. They say a good ship with a good crew is the best thing in the world.

3

The pro crew of the Corporation Caixagalica CXG *shows full participation in the MediCup off Alicante. Modern sponsoring should also motivate fellow workers, here the employees of the Galician Savings Banks, which sponsors this TP 52.*

Turning maneuvers on the South African America's Cup entrant Shosholoza. *On the foresheet, which could still be hauled by hand, there is now pressure; the grinder crew is cranking already. The faster the sail comes around, the less the muscle-men have to work.*

"To be a good helmsman, one has to have a certain instinct."

Karol Jablonski

Whether on an America's Cupper or a gaff cutter, in the cockpit of an IMS yacht or at the masthead, concentration and alertness are professional virtues. The smallest deviation can cost a victory; the cooperation of the crew must match to a fraction of a second in most maneuvers.

“They are a group of friends who sail with each other—and that is a strong combination, hard to assemble and very hard to beat.”

Prada *skipper Francesco de Angelis about the* Alinghi *crew.*

Markus Roy has the top job on the German America's Cupper United Internet Team Germany *(left page, right), Oliver Herledant is up high on* China Team. *The mast people are equipped like professional climbers and are lifted high on a fall; they run up the mast with it. As wind spotters, they observe the regatta stretch and the water at a great distance, so that the afterguard learns of wind-turners and breeze-holders. Communication with the cockpit, where things are noisy, is done via headphones.*

The bow before the spinnaker maneuver. On Alinghi *(at the UBS Trophy) everything is already clear; on* Corwel 45 *in Europrix training, it is being cleared up.*

Left page: A hard, wet job in a stormy mistral. In northern latitudes the crews would at least wear spraytops. – At the stern of the Oiseau de Feü, *the meticulously reconstructed* Firebird, *a visit during the regatta does not disturb them. It is safest there. – Center and right: The man at the bow has the same job on classics as on modern yachts: keep his eyes open and be quick about changing sails.*

"The one who can do it better subordinates himself."

Michael Illbruck after winning the Volvo Ocean Race, 2002-03.

A very promising greeting! The wives and girlfriends of the crew welcome their victors. At least the enthusiasm is genuine in this picture. The cupper crews rarely see their families during training, and after the competition a tremendous burden falls off the teams. There are a lot more people there than one normally sees on board. After the victory of America, *helpers and shore crew climb on deck while the ship is towed into harbor. [Look closely and you'll see that the mammoth mammaries are not genuine!]*

REGATTA

With the Wind and the Challenge

Below: Downwind and on the cross (right page). So much order can bring out egotism. Each of these crews knows only one goal: to bring themselves to the front and experience no disadvantages from the enemy. That leads to formations in which hordes of success-hungry sailors agitate like a great organism. The regatta field as a swarm.

If one gives sailors two boats, they have a race. Humanity is born to compete, the sporting spirit cannot be separated from the spirit. Even commercial sailors trim the sails unobtrusively when they are on the same course. Large sums were bet on the arrival of the wooden tea clippers in London, and a hundred years later the steel windjammers took part in their famous wheat race. Naturally, there were auction results for the tea clippers, but it was a matter of honor. Competition and playful measuring of strength are more than merely a human need; behavioral researchers observe it everywhere in nature. For the biology writer Bernd Heinrich, "racing" is a metaphor for living, joyful play and training for serious matters at the same time. Whether America's Cup or Cowes Week, Capetown or Kiel—Heinrich Hecht goes often and gladly to regattas.

The ships there are in their best form, the crews highly motivated, the parties legendary. When one talks of the "sailing scene," one always refers to regatta sailors. The high school of sailing is learned in a group, and then one works his way up until he meets a superior opponent.

Two variations of racing are common in sailing: the duel (match racing) and the start in the field. In fleet racing, one sails with either similar ships that go against each other evenly or is handicapped according to more or less complicated formulae that give a ship calculated to be inferior a time advantage.

In match racing it is just a matter of crossing the line ahead of your opponent. In sailing against many competitors, one must simply be the fastest of many. That calls for different characters in the cockpit.

C45
SWE
8799
INVESTOR
www.investor.se
FRA
883
MALLORCA
yachting
MALLORCA yachting
GBR
4545R
FRA
18043

The helmsmen and tacticians, who are taken on board for important races, are called "hired guns" by the Americans. The successful Jochen Schümann, who won and defended the America's Cup with the *Alinghi* team, declines such individual engagements, because for him thorough joint preparation of a team, training with the whole crew, is an essential factor for success.

In match racing too, a fast boat and a trained crew are half the battle, but above all it is a matter of tactically correct sailing and watching the opponent from the start, if possible. But being faster than the opponent can also mean willingly sailing more slowly than one actually could, just to prevent the other from getting away on a lucky turn of wind.

Whoever gets into a duel in a big regatta field has already lost. While two ships have a private duel, the competitors sail past unhindered.

Regattas usually take place far from the public. One cannot see much from land. Whoever wants to photograph regattas, does it from a motorboat, a helicopter, or—as Heinrich Hecht did for the photo on page 124—from a church steeple.

Victory by size? In the 1988 America's Cup off San Diego, the "dinosaur" New Zealand *of banker Michael Fay (left) lost—Seaworthy racers in the 2000 One Ton Cup off Marseilles.*

ADVANCED COMPOSITES

After 15 years off the high seas, Udo Schutz's most modern "Container" to date, an STP 65 (left page). The carbon-aramide fabric material, which the lettering on the boom advertises, is made in the owner's factory. The material is also used in airbus planes and high-tech yachts. – Photos below (from left): Shamoun *before the citadel of Saint-Tropez. – The American Maxis* Numbers *(owner Jim Schwartz) and* Moneypenny *(Dan Meyer) with the Italian* Swan 42 *(Leonardo Ferragamo) at the Voiles de Saint-Tropez—The star super-J class yacht* Ranger, *a copy of Vanderbilt's cup defender. On the megayacht* Hebridean Spirit, *up to 110 VIPs enjoy ringside seats on the sea.*

Alinghi *and* Team Emirates New Zealand *in the Louis Vuitton Cup off Valencia in 2007. For the New Zealander, it was an elimination round for the challenge, For the Swiss a test of strength against potential competitors in the America's Cup. They actually met again on the New Zealander and defended the cup.*

USA
25555
RAMBLER

SUI 75
UBS
NZL84
Fly Emirates

The maxi-yacht Rambler *won the overall victory in the 2008 Maxi Rolex Cup. In this series of major-league racing, about 40 ships competed in six size classes. –* Senso One *(ex-*Mari Cha IV*) is the world's fastest schooner, up to 40 knots in a sprint, 147-foot [45 meter] high masts. With six days, 17 hours, and 52 minutes, the 147-foot yacht almost cut Charlie Barr's hundred-year-old Atlantic record in half.*

"I set few standards in the pre-start phase, am fairly complicated for the opponent."

Karol Jablonski.

USA25
GER
4414
USA-50036
ndia Life Cowes Week

Left page: A temple of sailing sport, The Castle, *the club house of the Royal Yacht Squadron next to Trinity Church in Cowes. – Below: The Admiral's Cup, from the scarcely less prestigious Royal Ocean Racing Club, is one of the most coveted sailing trophies among high-seas sailors. In the removable base, coins from 1958 are hidden. The memorial tablet (small photo at right) remembers the 19 sailors who were lost in the Fastnet race for the Admiral's Cup in 1979.*

The Yacht Squadron has 365 members. The only Germans in the club are the three-time Admiral's Cup winner, "Sir" Hans-Otto Schümann and, in his day, Kaiser Wilhelm II. The club is a civilian branch of the Navy, since Nelson's flag officer Hardy joined the founding committee and club members offered their yachts to the crown as fast couriers and surveillance ships. Princess Anne (right, next to Willi Illbruch) honored the club with her presence as chairperson of the British Sailors' Organization.

At the start of the 605-mile Fastnet Race, the helmsmen don't waste a second. Whoever messes up the start needs hours to work his way back to the front—or loses contact. Jameson *falls off to find a better current nearer to land. Hecht took this photo from the Trinity Church steeple.*

"Not when I play it."

W. C. Fields to the question of whether poker is a game of chance.

Left: The America's Cup, the world's most famous sailing trophy, seen in San Diego in 1988 before the prize was awarded. The English donated the 100 Guineas Cup on the occasion of the 1851 World's Fair and lost it to the schooner America. *Despite many attempts, they never won it back. The flag in the background is that of the New Zealand challenger. The cup remained in the USA. – Above:* Luna Rossa Challenge *did not qualify for the final in 2007, but dropped out in the Louis Vuitton Cup. Seven years before, the Italian challenger* Luna Rossa *lost to the defender,* New Zealand, *by half a second.*

Louis Vuitton, Act 12, qualification race for the 32nd America's Cup in Valencia, 2007. Team New Zealand *in a match race with* Alinghi. *They sailed the same way in the finale, with the Swiss defending the cup successfully.*

Team New Zealand *against* Young America, *which was entered in the race by the Stars & Stripes syndicate, although it had lost in the elimination race. The Kiwis won 5 to nothing.*

Hook striking and circling – before the start it is in the rules of match racing that one seeks the position at the other's stern to be able to watch him. Whoever is in front tries to shake off his pursuer. Whoever can maneuver better, keep more way on the ship and sail faster wins the starting duel.

The French Areva Challenge *at the windward buoy. As the 18th man on board, the rules allow a guest, who may not leave his seat at the stern during the race.*

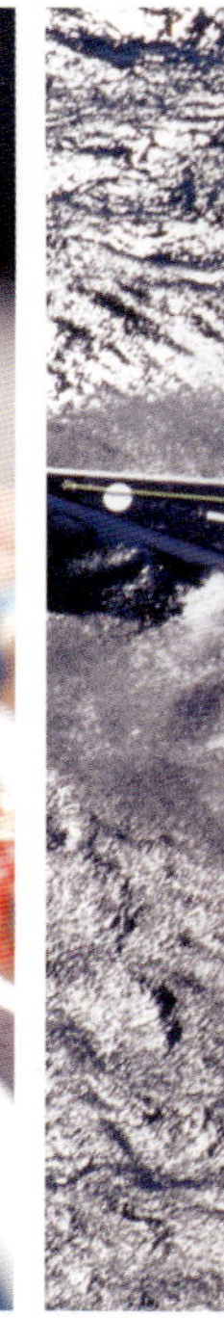

Valencia, 2007: To offer the public more of a show (and the sponsors more publicity), the America's Cuppers sailed not only matches but also fleet races. – A simple magnetic compass on BMW Oracle*. Even on an electrically equipped racing yacht there can be a power failure. Besides, it is practical and ... simply belongs on every ship.*

BMW Oracle *in the UBS Trophy off Newport. A look into the cockpit from above reveals how slim the IACC yachts are with their 14.75-foot [4.50-meter] breadth.* – Emirates New Zealand *ahead of* Alinghi. *The pursuer tries to take the wind from the leading ship. The men on the masts cannot see each other.*

"The America's Cup should take place more on the water and not so much on land. It is unfortunately often forgotten that it is a sailing regatta."

Russell Coutts

Left page: A sharp wedge weighing 24 tons, Alinghi *at the 2004 UBSD Trophy off Newport. –* Stars and Stripes *won the last race against the gigantic* New Zealand, *and the Americans let the corks pop. It is not so much a sporting victory that is to be celebrated after this mismatch of completely unlike boats, but the end of a legal battle that the judge moved out of the courtroom onto the water. "First go and sail," she decided; then we'll see if it was a "fair and even match." As a result, Dennis Conner tried to sail faster, but not noticeably faster, than the Kiwi cruiser. While the crew was still celebrating, the International America's Cup Class (IACC) was basically decided.*

N37WA

ORACLE

Left page: BMW Oracle *in the wind and on the spinnaker. So that there would be a little difference in the pictures despite the dearth of wind, photographers flew into the picture from opposite sides in their chartered helicopters. – Right page: The Spanish team,* Desafio Espanol, *sailed in the 2007 Louis Vuitton Cup (here in Act 12) remarkably successfully. It was beaten only in the semi-final by the New Zealanders who then won the final and appeared against the defender,* Alinghi. *The America's Cup certainly awakens national sentiments, but has been for a long time, like other top-line sports, a very international event. A German, Jochen Schümann, and a troupe of New Zealanders around national hero Russell Coutts had won the cup from New Zealand in 2003 for the Swiss Bertarelli, bringing the cup back to Europe, which did not please the New Zealanders at all. The Spanish boat was steered by Karol Jablonski, a German with Polish roots, which did not please the Spanish press. The further forward the Spaniards moved in the Louis Vuitton acts, the more the fans liked Jablonski, who had formerly contracted with Poles and an Italian team for financial relief, and then had signed with the unsuccessful German team.*

Left page: Alinghi *and* BMW Oracle *maneuver for the better starting position: In the UBS Trophy of 2004, held off Newport, the Americans won both the series of pro-driver competitions plus the owners' races, in which Larry Ellison and Ernesto Bertarelli steered. – Above: The first impression betrays, but the scene did not take place in the USA, rather in Australia, in Fremantle harbor. Heinrich Hecht photographed the American fans in a whirl of joy after Dennis Conner, the Australian, had taken the America's Cup again.*

Left: The bow man of the Italian Mascalzone Latinö *had a wet job. – Center: After every race the hull of* BMW Oracle *was cleaned. An IACC yacht may carry 19 tons of ballast. – Right:* United Internet Team Germany *gained experience mainly off Valencia and took the next-to-last place before China.*

The bow of the +39 Challenge *dips into the wake of* BMW Oracle*, but after that the Italians stayed on course. The Americans turned shortly thereafter to keep their pursuer in sight. A ground rule says, "Stay between your opponent and the windward buoy."*

Six men in unison: For a photo like this work-study at the Admiral's Cup, a position on the windward buoy is best suited. Corum *falls away and has its spinnaker clear.*

America's cup 1992, San Diego. America *beat* Il Moro di Venezia *by a three-second lead in a weak wind. This finish was, until then, the closest finale in the cup's history.*

MEAN MACHINE

Left page, left: The man on the mast—everyday life on a modern regatta ship. A member of the deck crew is always equipped with a boatswain's chair, which has changed slowly into a comfortable climber's chair. – Right: Mean Machine *in the Admiral's Cup; the crew prepares the goosenecks and the shifting of the spinnakers. –Right page: Without a rail and a bow pulpit, and with a sharp stem sticking far forward, the slim America's Cuppers are reminiscent of classic racing yachts. Now their era is also past.*

Audi
BREITLING
MEDCUP

Left page, left: TP 52 at the Breitling Audi MedCup of 2007; the photos were taken off Mallorca and Alicante, at right. Stay Calm *in the Spinnaker maneuver.—Right page: The Spanish Siemens before the British* Cristabella *– The spinnaker boom is in place, everything is ready for the headwind move. – The foreshipman signals the cockpit crew the distance to to the starting line, then the contest begins. The TransPac 52s were created on the American Pacific coast, but enjoy great popularity in Europe. The elite of sea sailors are regularly, or occasionally, traveling on TP 52s. When the 2007 America's Cup was once again at the mercy of lawyers, many crews switched to TP 52s.*

EUR
GER
4540
GER-4540

Left page: Three Maxis of the Fastnet fleet at the Needles, the 98-foot [30-meter] chalk cliffs at the west end of the Isle of Wight. From the Solent they sail out to Fastnet Rock on the south coast of Ireland and back to Cowes. For Morning Glory, Nicorette, *and* Intrum Justitia *(from front) the 605 miles in a good wind become a two-day trip; the greater part of the fleet is away three days or longer. They are made for long stretches in day races. Above: TP 52* Onö *at the Breitling MedCup off Alicante.*

M 36
GER 4293
DAIMLER BE

Left page: The beginning of systematically sponsored high-sea sailing in Germany. The Mumm 36 Aerosail *started at the Kiel Week in 1995, and this large-scale sport project served to build up a high-sea cadre and develop suitable material. Daimler-Benz had found in sailing the "clean" kind of sport that looked good with a technological company. – Below left: The One Ton Cup off Marseilles. –Right: A good trip with a weak evening breeze. Maxis with spinnakers sail into the bay at Saint-Tropez.*

"It is not said in vain that the America's Cup is not an auction. Money and time alone are not enough; it depends on having the right people do the right thing."

Jochen Schümann

Steered by American John Kostecki, Illbruck was the first German yacht to win the Volvo Ocean Race in 2002. Kiel prepared an enthusiastic welcome for the green 60-foot racer in the firth, where 50,000 sailors awaited her.

Breitling MedCup 2007, off Alicante. Anonimo Q8, Siemens *(ESP), and* Platoon *on the way to the course marker; the Russians (at right) can fall back. At once the spinnakers go up and the first crew members spring into their positions.*

"Between the seas we suddenly saw a yacht come out from behind the rocks; it must have turned near the surf. It was the *Magistri*, as we soon confirmed. In our opinion, an irresponsible maneuver, but that's how people sail today."

Rubin navigator Mike Iwand about Fastnet 1979.

In the Swan World Cup the Hissar *(above) and the British Swan 60 R* Highland Fling *– not to be confused with the German yacht of the same name – run into the bay of Porto Cervo. The wild rocky coast of the Costa Smeralda is a Mecca of the high-sea regatta scene and the showplace of many highly ranked regattas in the Mediterranean.*

Highland Fling

In the Nioulargue, the mast of Albatross *came down. The crew goes about the cleaning-up work with concentration and without haste. First the loose pieces of wood have to be cut loose or secured, so that no further damage takes place. Other yachts come to help.*

Morning Glory *at Rothmans' Week off Capetown. The cloud-blanketed Table Mountain and the big city where the Atlantic and Indian Oceans meet is the setting for an expressive sailing array. The Cape of Good Hope was originally called "Cape of Storms."*

Longobarda, *built in 1989, at the Maxi World Cup off Saint-Tropez. The 80-foot ships were originally conceived as high-sea yachts and were then bought by rich and very rich people as Spartan day sailers. The crews—up to 27 men—stayed overnight on land.*

Three yacht generations later: The TP 52s were originally conceived as high-sea yachts and then converted to day sailers by wealthy people. Cape Mediterrano *is 28 feet shorter than* Longobarda *and usually much faster than the Maxis were twenty years ago.*

GBR
93R

Super-yachts off Saint-Tropez. They meet here at the end of the Mediterranean season before going across the Atlantic and to the south. The 140 foot [42.6-meter] schooner Senso One *(center) has improved the 100-year-old Atlantic record by two and a half days, to 9 days, 15 hours, 55 minutes, as the* Mari-Cha IV.

MLT 55
Senso one

RUSAL
BREITLING MEDCUP
novoship
SYNERGY
TIMMERMAN YACHTS
SOVCOMFLOT
RUSAL SYNERGY

Left page: Highly concentrated work happens on Rusal Synergy. *The Russians are newcomers to TP 52. The new ship won two long stretches in the Middle Sea Race, sailed in the later MedCup Race, but finished in the middle third. – Harm Müller-Spreers'* Platoon *comes from Germany and won the bronze at the 2008 WM.*

SAILOR

The Human Factor

Jochen Schümann at the tiller of his 36-foot [11-meter] One-Design at the Aerosol Project; beside him is Bernd Zirkelbach. Schümann was the sports director, Zirkelbach the trainer of this thrust project sponsored by Mercedes-Benz, for German high-sea sailing. For this picture, Hecht climbed up the mast. – You are the greatest, darling.
Right: America's Cup veteran Paul Cayard (five participations, two victories) with his wife Icka, Swedish by birth, in Southampton. He had just won the 1998 Whitbread Round The World Race with the Swedish EF Language.

Sailing is not purely a sport for prominent people. As a photographer, one meets a great many people on the water and in the clubs, people the tabloids are interested in. Great yachts are unaffordable for the little guy, so they must be paid for by rich people (or sponsors) and crewed by good sailors, who also want to be paid.

The great yachting sport draws people like the software billionaire Larry Ellison; it is a playground for crowned heads and uncrowned princes. The most exclusive yacht club in the world, the Royal Yacht Squadron in Cowes, is allowed to fly the battle flag, the White Ensign, instead of the red British commercial flag. The club's founders had placed their fast yachts at the service of the crown at times, and above all it was blessed by inviting King George VI into the boat as its commodore. The scene is legendary in which Queen Victoria in 1851, after the race around the Isle of Wight, inquired who had finished second. The *America,* a schooner from the heretical overseas provinces, had humbled the entire British yacht fleet. "There is no second, Madam," an officer is said to have growled. With this race the story of the America's Cup began. The Americans honored the stubborn donor, Sir Thomas Lipton, who had challenged five times without success, with a cup of his own. The steadfast Englishman, though, was no loser, for all America now drank his tea and made the man rich.

When Kaiser Wilhelm II let his splendid *Meteor* cruise off Cowes in the summer of 1892, the heir to the British throne ordered his mega-yacht *Britannia.*

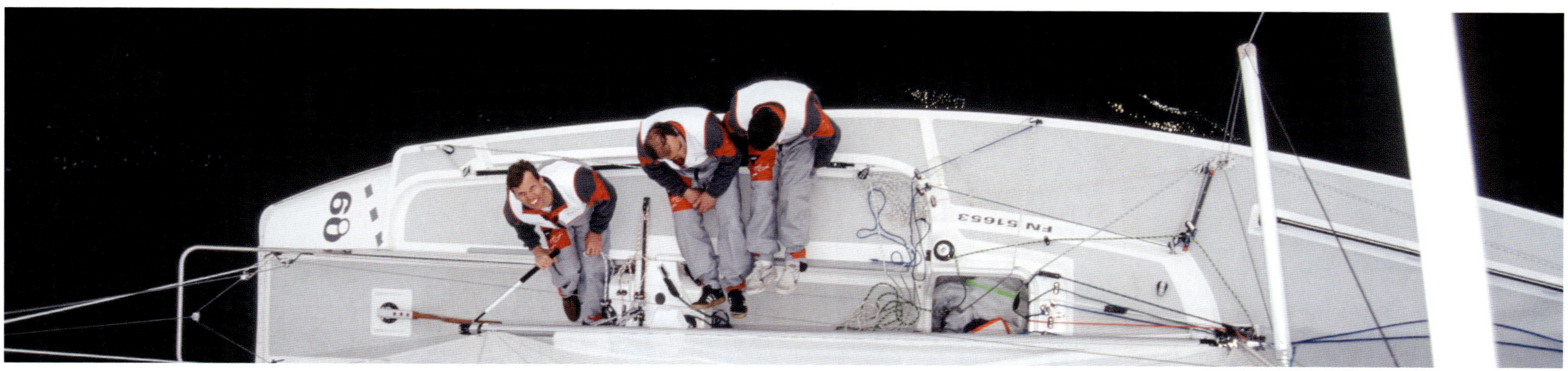

Not even a hundred years later, Prince Luitpold of Bavaria good-naturedly dealt with Kiel policemen who took offense at the Bavarian flag on his star class boat. Really great names often honor their sport in really small boats. For the higher nobility, at sea and over beer before the victor was honored, it was a case of "Here you are a human being, here you may be one."

The yachting sport is a playground for the elite, however one defines them. Talents are discovered and encouraged, the parties are for kings and festivals for the nouveau riche are a carnival of vanity. And the real celebrities on the scene are sailors, who have gained notice for their achievements. Practically all the stars have gained their ability in great regatta fields in small boats. They have worked their way upward without compulsion and became "in" at some time, thanks to their ability. On every first-class regatta yacht one finds former Olympians and national champions, at least.

The owners of the top yachts are mostly successful business people or artists. Karajan directed his ship and crew like an orchestra; only the most necessary words were spoken on board. Business people, monarchs, and politicians have their working style on land, and on board it turns out that this is also their lifestyle.

Left page: The Hollander Bouwe Bekking (here with the 1999 Admiral's Cup) is one of the most successful European high-sea sailors. He sailed around the world five times, won a dozen international races, including Sydney-Hobart and the Capetown-Rio race three times.

Hasso Plattner traveled from San Francisco for the Capetown-Rio Race. His crew expected that he would first want to rest a bit after the long trip, but he preferred to ignore the jet-lag in training on the sea.

Left: Tops in 470s: Daria Blaschkiewitz (on left) and Geeske Genrich won the Women's Junior European Championship in 2005 by avoiding a duel with their opponents, who had equal points, in the last run and sailing their own race.

Tears of joy at the finish. The Norwegian Linda Andersen sailed to Olympic gold off Barcelona in Europe. Of the boat, one sees only the sheet and tiller.

GER

After three gold medals, Jochen Schümann wins "only" silver while sailing off Sydney, with Gunnar Bahr and Ingo Borkowski (far left). Germany's most successful sailor is seen before the Royal Yacht Squadron in Cowes, with Thomas Friese and Tony Gayle ("MKKP"). – Above: Souvenir photo of the skipper at the 1999 One Ton Club off Majorcia. Beside Schümann is Crown Prince Felipe of Spain. At right: The heir to the throne steered the Alfos. *Other than Hecht, no photographer was allowed on board.*

Above left: King Harald of Norway at the rudder of Fram XV. *The monarch is an enthusiastic sailor who also takes the wheel with friends or lends his own ship. Right: Prince Henrik of Denmark, husband of Queen Margrethe II, sails sportingly and traditionally. Left: His tiller acrobatics in the cockpit of the dragon are worth seeing.*

Right: Denmark's Crown Prince Fredrik in his dragon. Sport sailing in an open keelboat is the private and, in Denmark, very down-to-earth pleasure of monarchs. – Below right: Sailing ace Poul-Richard Hoj-Jensen (on left) with the heir to the throne having a beer before the yacht club. – Below left: Well, how was it with you? Juan Carlos, King of Spain, chats after the competition with Felipe, Prince of the Asturias. Heinrich Hecht met the father and son at Mallorca for the 2007 Breitling MedCup.

Tatzelwurm

Left page: Prince Ludwig of Bavaria with Gregor and Benedikt Franke on his Dragon Tatzelwurm. – *The name is that of a legendary little dragon known only in the Alpine area.*

Upper left: Tim Kröger aboard the Whitbread racer Swedish Match. *Right: Kröger is one of the few German full professionals on the high-sea yacht scene. Journalist Tatjana Pohorny wrote about him regularly. The man she got to know in the process pleased her more and more, and now they are married.*

Heinrich Hecht picks up Dennis Conner at Hamburg airport for the first Baltic Match Race, and naturally takes a small photo at passport check. Right: In 1987 he made his breakthrough as a professional photographer with his picture of Conner's champagne shower. – Below: Conner already had the license plate "DC in 91" made in 1988, before his victory over the New Zealand challenger, as a battle cry for the next cup campaign. –Right page: Conner is training with the rigid-wing catamaran Stars & Stripes. *He mastered the complicated boat perfectly.*

S.D.Y.C.

Beautiful women, great ships, and one of the greatest designers: German Frers (above, at the rudder) has designed high-sea yachts for decades; they win races and later become classics. From the first Whitbread victor, a Swan 65, to the modern Wallys and Volvo Ocean 70s, the Argentinian's office guarantees strong and fast ships.

"You are a liar!"

New Zealand designer Bruce Farr in 1988, before journalists, to John Marshall, the designer of Conner's catamaran Stars & Stripes.

"You are a loser; disappear!"

Dennis Conner to Bruce Farr, reacting to the word "liar."

Above left: Börge Börresen (died 2007) built, at the shipyard in Vejle, 325 of those wooden dragons that are called the most beautiful in the world, but he also helped to establish the plastic dragons. For fifty years he did not miss a Gold Cup; finally, at the age of 74, he became world champion (with his son Ole and Jesper Bank). – Center: The model Tatjana Patitz decorates the rudder of *BMW Oracle*. –Right: Harold Cudmore on not-so-good a day. He had just sunk, in his home area off the Trish coast, the yacht that he had borrowed from the King of Norway. Friends suspected that the press would call him "Jameson on the rocks" the next day (the whisky brewer was the boat's sponsor), but the headline read, "Sorry, Majesty, I sank your yacht."

"The New York Yacht Club has gained a flying start among its challengers. They have in Bruce Farr the unchallenged best designer in the world."

Dennis Conner in an interview before the 2002-03 America's Cup in New Zealand.

Left page: Hans-Otto Schümann, recognizable by his black Elbe-sailor cap, at the rudder of his Rubin XIV. *He won the Admiral's cup three times and the Sardinia's Cup twice with the German team – his ships are always called* Rubin *(ruby). Nine years after World War II he took part in Cowes Week as the first German to do so. The Britons showed respect to the friendly German by inducting him into the royal Yacht Squadron. The German press ennobled him as "Sir Schümann." – Above left: Thomas Friese with his daughter Alexandra and far outside on the high edge of his* Tina i-Punkt. *Friese also trains, if need be, in the freezing temperatures on the river Elbe.*

The nautical heroes of New Zealand, Peter Blake and Russell Coutts, after the America's Cup victory in 1995. Blake–in the top right photo with his wife Pippa and son James—sailed five Whitbread races, was the first to sail around the world in fewer than 80 days, and was knighted by the Queen. On an expedition on the Amazon, robbers shot him. – Left: Russell Coutts, who would rather shower others with champagne than be showered himself, clowned with his countrymen when he won with the Swedish Alinghi *team and beat* Emirates Team New Zealand *five to two. Right: He also cuts a good figure as a Dragon sailor.*

The Helgolander professional sailor Ralph Steitz has been high up in international business since the early 1980s. He is the first German to sail in the America's Cup—even though the defense with Young America *ended with a 0 to 5 defeat by the New Zealanders.*

A great man in a small boat, Karol Jablonski won the Audi Streamline Match Race from a standstill. Many consider him Germany's best match racer (and surely the best ice sailor). He led the Spanish America's Cup team Defiaso *2007 surprisingly until the semi-final of the Louis Vuitton Cups. The Danziger's German career began when he, because of too much contact with the West, fled from the Polish national cadre. He went to relatives in Germany and finally, through a shipyard job on the Steinhuder Meer, got into a professional sailor's career. Jablonski (with son Kaspar at Cowes) won with the German team in the 1993 Admiral's Cup (in* Container*) and finished second in 1995.*

Lawrence Joseph "Larry" Ellison steers his BMW Oracle *in the UBS Trophy. The software entrepreneur has developed his Data Bank Systems to a 25 billion dollars fortune and fourteenth place on the Forbes list of the world's richest people. On board it is said that the difference between Larry Ellison and God is that God does not think He is Larry Ellison.*

Karim Aga Khan IV is known to sailors as the man who discovered the Costa Smeralda, the Emerald Coast, in northern Sardinia and built Porto Cervo, the sailors' paradise. Actually the descendant of the Prophet is a very versatile man. As a sportsman, industrialist, and promoter of large humanitarian projects in Europe and the Orient, he enjoys high respect.

Helmut Jahn—photographed by Heinrich Hecht in 1998—is as ambitious a sailor as an architect. He studied in Munich and Chicago, where he got to know Mies van der Rohe. His futuristic State of Illinois Center gave him the nickname of "Flash Gordon." Jahn, among whose best-known buildings are the Sony Center with the railroad tower in Berlin, the new airport in Bangkok, and the Frankfurt Fair Tower, is one of the world's most in-demand architects. At the Rolex Farr 40 World Championship off Newport he won the first races, steering the on-wind courses himself and leaving the before-wind stretches to his son Evan.

FLASH GORDON

Jörg Diesch is one of the few German Olympic winners (Flying Dutchman, 1976) and a world champion in sailing. At the rudder of Peter Westphal-Langloh's Formula I racer Hawesta *he took second place in the Grand Prix and won 25,000 dollars (ahead of Berend Beilken and Dennis Conner).*

Doug Petersen designs victorious yachts like Black Magic *and privately sails his 29.5-foot [9-meter] R-yacht* Tamara IX*, a Christian Jensen design of 1933.—Above right: Petra Niemann joined the Berlin Seglerhaus club on the Wannsee as a nine-year-old (to which Finn idol Willi Kuhweide belongs) and sailed in the Olympic Games in Sydney and Athens. –Below left: Bill Koch rejoices in camp after a victory by* America*, which beat the challenger* Il Moro di Venezia *four to one. – Far right: King Constantine of Greece with the organizer of the Dragon Jubilee Regatta, Chris Dicker.*

Harro Kniffka (1956-2009) is known to sailors as the "godfather the Dragon." The Bremen shipowner, born in Rostock, definitely contributed to the renaissance of the elegant keelboats by founding the "Hanseatic Lloyd Dragon Grand Prix."

Kniffka got to know Heinrich Hecht through Ulli Libor when he was looking for a photographer for the Dragon Jubilee. "That was the beginning of a friendship that does not exist often," says the photographer. The photo on this side shows Harro Kniffka, along with Olympic winner Ulli Libor and IOC President Jacques Rogge, steering his dragon off Saint-Tropez.

With these photos Heinrich Hecht says farewell to his friend. Harro Kniffka suffered from cancer and died in April 2009, while this book was being assembled.

In a strong wind off Saint-Tropez, from left: Harro Kniffka, Ulli Libor, Jacques Rogge.

On his yacht Maranatha.

WIND

... and No Wind

Stillness over the water; the way home can be very long. Good if one has time and can enjoy the evening (below). – Right page: In the 2005 Dragon Championship off Neustadt the wind blew nicely. With winds from south-west to north, the bay is protected. Only when the wind turns farther to the east is the seaway rough.

The driving power for sailors is created by sunshine. The temperature differences in the air lead to different pressures, the speed difference between the water surface and the atmosphere is wind. The resistance created by the boat opposes the wind and may be converted into drive. The ship hurries until the moving resistance is as great as the driving power of the wind.

Many laymen find it hard to understand that a ship can sail faster than the wind is blowing. Sport catamarans, surfers, and ice sailors prove, though, that this works very well in practice. What matters on board is the "apparent" wind, that is a combination of the "real" and the traveling wind and becomes stronger with increasing motion. The driving energy of the wind accumulates.

Wind is hard to photograph, for it is invisible. No wind is even harder to photograph, and only results certainly justify the trick which Heinrich Hecht employed in the calm at Valencia (page 202). The photo of the foreshipman who wrote "no wind" on the soles of his feet at Hecht's request is one of Hecht's most published pictures. Newspapers, TV stations, and agencies all over the world wanted photos of America's Cup, but one race after another was called off for lack of wind. The seekers at the masthead who supply their skippers with information about wind fields, could stay on deck.

Wind has many names: the mistral, meltemi, and bora bora are local winds, the passate are a global system. When Coriolis described the power named after him, one understood how the earth's rotation made gigantic swirls of air arise.

DEN
355
D
IRL
174
D
SWE
311
D
RUS
77

People and ships live in an unstable element. They are subjected to gentle and powerful influences, and they want to see their achievements recognized and not their weaknesses exposed.

Joseph Conrad, The Mirror of the Sea

Low-pressure areas move counter-clockwise in the Northern Hemisphere and clockwise in the Southern. The big low regions grow out of countless local systems. Coastal sailors know the "sea wind," a thermic wind that arises on sunny mornings and is strongest in early afternoon. All the world's sailing regions—naturally also inland—have their wind qualities, and good sailors know and use them.

The English Admiral Beaufort established a wind-strength scale because the log-book prose of his captains was too imprecise. The Beaufort scale extends from a breeze (Bft. 1) to a gale (11) and a fully grown hurricane (12). Sailors still use this scale today. Regatta sailors state wind speeds in sea miles per hour (knots). At 64 knots the wind strength's 12th range begins.

The air in a calm weather can be threatening and oppressive, the spring wind from the northeast icy, the turning wind at the finish line can be nasty. Amateurs occasionally notice that they need to explain in private or with the slide projector off what a picture actually shows. A professional cannot do that. He does not know the viewers of his pictures.

Hecht has photographed from a helicopter in storm squalls that endangered the helicopter, while the crew below him sailed in shorts and T-shirts. One sees the one, not the other. There are the thousand unnoticed details that let us sailors know that in the picture there is wind, and why it was blowing.

The power of the wind is passed from sails to sheets, lines, and masts. The mast of this 20-foot [6-meter] yacht Clymene II *broke. Material failure or misuse? The wind strength alone was not the problem, as the other boats show.*

Right page: The travel yacht moves with too much pressure and heel. A smaller foresail or a second reef in the mainsail would help the ship move better. This page: Aschanti IV, *on the other hand, is in its element in a strong wind.*

Left: Star boats are over-tackled and cannot be reefed; a squall like this on a Kiel Week is weathered with a killing stern leech. – This page: For one-man boats like Europes and Contenders, a strong wind is no problem if the sailor puts enough weight on the balance and is quick about trimming. After tipping, the boat is quickly righted again.

"One needs a heavy boat for races in the spring and a light one for the semi-finals."

Dennis Conner

Left: A spinnaker maneuver on Corum *at the Kiel Week. Heinrich Hecht chartered the helicopter to photograph for the sponsor – Above:* Noddy *in need. The ship has run out of its rudder, but the helmsman will soon have it back under control.*

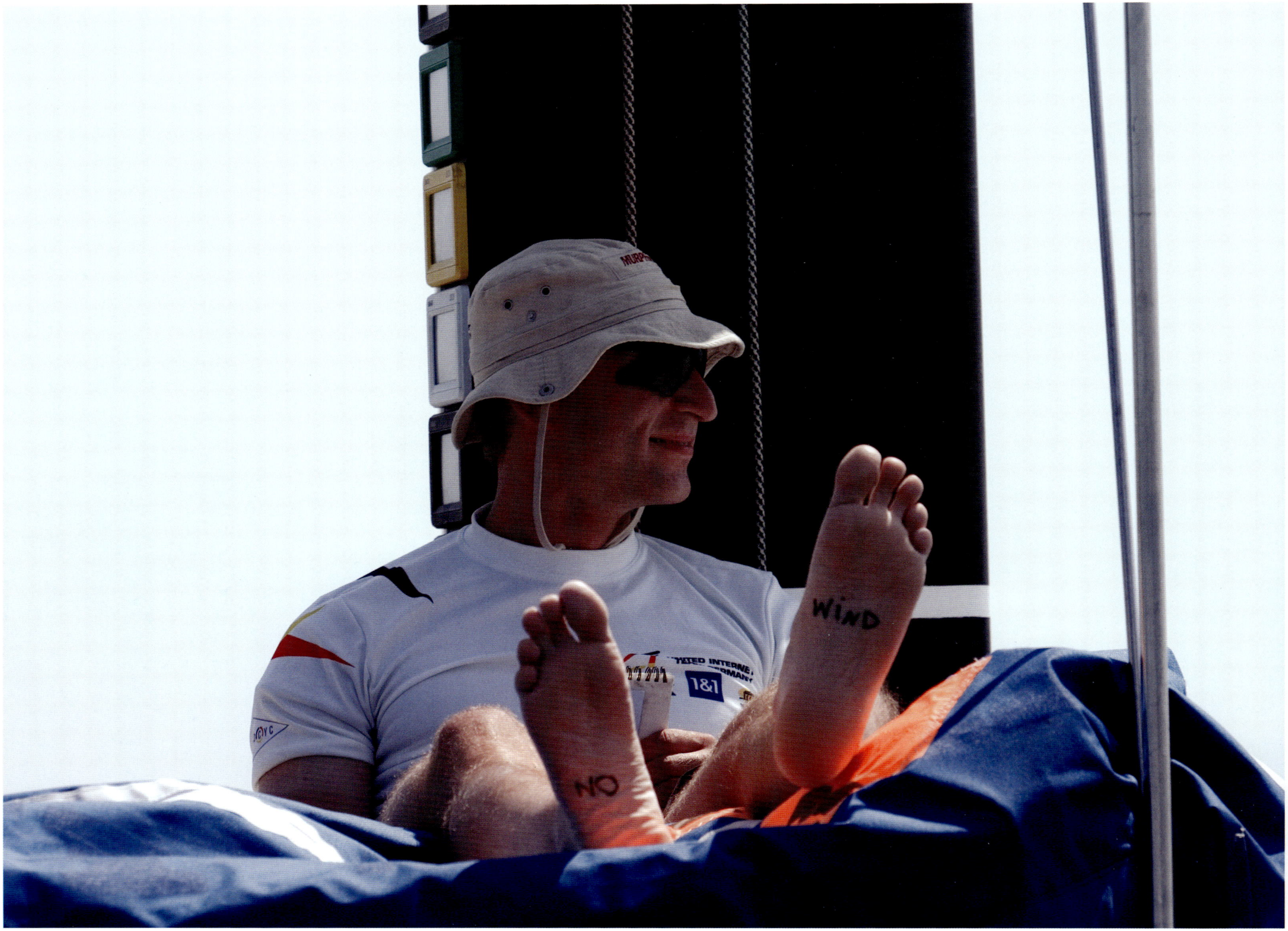
WIND
NO
1&1

Left page: Heinrich Hecht was at the 2007 America's Cup eliminations as the team photographer for the German syndicate. After several calm days he asked the pitman, Jan Schoepe, at breakfast for a small favor. "If you cannot sail, write it..." The calm got on people's nerves, but that is also part of sport.

"In my position I am privileged in life and am much regarded by the people, but the wind takes no particular notice of me. Everybody is treated equally by the wind."

King Harald V of Norway

94 R
S2

Left: The Wallys Magic Carpet *and* Indio *sail a private match race off Cassis in a calm. Under these conditions being less slow than one's opponent requires fingertip feeling when steering and trimming the sails. The mega yachts have it no easier than the 49ers at Travemünde Week.*

Left page: A Caribbean tornado with a strong wind! Even as the skipper of a private yacht, Heinrich Hecht reaches for his camera.

Concentrated light-wind sailing on the Baltic Sea at MAIOR 2008. The crew, threatened by the wind shadow of the weathering pursuer, has no time to see the beauty of the scene.

BLACK & WHITE

Contrast Program

Since good color film has existed, black-and-white photography has had a hard life. For portraits and architecture, artistic and journalistic photography, it was the first choice for a long time, but since even the rotary presses of the great newspapers have printed in color, black-and-white pictures have been practically unsaleable on the market.

Heinrich Hecht also produces almost exclusively in color (and almost always digitally). But sometimes he sees mental black-and-white pictures, and then he puts old-fashioned black-and-white film in his large-format camera. Thus result pictures that are impressions rather than actual color views of reality. Contrasts and smooth progressions of brightness can be seen without color, but unusually three-dimensionally. Hecht's black-and-white panoramas are strikingly sharp, and they reach an extent that might be lost in color.

Sometimes Heinrich Hecht goes so far as to switch to a "contrast program" afterward. Then he scans pictures in black-and-white. The cost is only a secondary concern. A black-and-white calendar is printed today on the same presses as a color calendar, and the preparation of the printing plates is no longer a concern. No, the viewpoints are aesthetic.

The human eye sees in black and white under certain conditions. At night all waves are gray. We sailors preserve the night-vision ability of the vision cells in the iris when we are on deck and see red night light instead of white light. It takes an hour before the eye adapts to the darkness and gets by with little light.

At the Audi MedCup off Alicante, European elite crews start who want to sail the regatta with TP 52 racers without pay. In the foreground on Bribon (Ne'er-do-well) *is the Spanish King Juan Carlos. Hecht took the picture with a 6 x 17 camera with wide angle lenses.*

Changing from color vision to "black-and-white" happens without effort; we scarcely notice it. Photos like those by Heinrich Hecht impress us through their depth. They let shapes move into the foreground where we are accustomed to colors.

"The America's Cup should remain the most important event in sailing sport. That will only happen if the most beautiful and technically most refined yachts take part."

Russell Coutts

The starting line of the MedCup fleet. All the ships want to create a "zero start." On the front end of the line, slightly favored by the wind, it is too tight, at the rear there is plenty of space. The photo gets its tremendous depth from the coastal mountains just visible in the fog.

Cintra, *the oldest sailing twelver, was designed, like so many classic yachts, by Scotsman William Fife III. It rotted away in the mud of the Thames thirty years ago before it was discovered by "treasure hunters" of the Camper & Nicholson shipyard. Italian enthusiasts restored the ship.*

"It is the art of fighting for a good position in the one or two minutes before the start by blocking one's direct opponent to the windward and creating free space to the leeward. If this succeeds, one can fall off and build up speed just before the starting gun."

Markus Wieser, tactician, IMS world champion, European dragon champion, multiple German champion.

Antoine Gallimard (FRA 335) with his dragon Feu-Follet *off Saint-Tropez. The dragon is seen by many as the most elegant open keel yacht that was ever built in series. Not without cause, the three-man boat is more attractive than ever after 75 years.*

U10 U10

The prelude to the 32nd America's Cup off Valencia, the Louis Vuitton Cup, Act 11. The Emirates Team New Zealand *(left), which finally won out as the challenger, in a match race with the American* BMW Oracle.

LOUIS
VUITTON

NZL
48
NEW ZEALAND
NEW ZEALAND
USA 8
BMW ORACLE Racing

WAVE

The Swing of the Sea

Swans push their way through the waves on the Costa Smeralda. On the Mediterranean, thanks to the deep water, waves quickly reach a considerable height (below). Above all, on the crossing one is going to get wet. The photo at right, that looks so Mediterranean because of the "nice" weather, was taken on the English Channel, which is a rough place to sail because of its steep waves.

Boats rock on the transition from the thick medium of water to the 800 times thinner medium of air. It is more rarely that the air rests and the water moves; the rule is: The wind blows over the water and creates waves. The wave scene goes from the first ripples on the smooth surface to the gigantic waves of the free-swinging ocean.

Boats must deal with these waves; they create waves themselves with their movement. It is a popular game at regattas to place yourself on the stern wave of a bigger, faster ship and, surfing on this wave, to profit from the achievement of the faster ship. Often a whole horde of small running-board riders travels on the wave system of a big ship.

There are waves that make yachts capsize, supported by the wind. When waves move from deep water into shallow, they build up. Somewhat different rules apply to the tsunami than to the Grundsee off Bagenkop. The normal seaway begins to form a surf wave when, on a rising ocean floor, the water depth is only half as much as the distance between the wave crests.

Waves crest. That means at a 160-foot [fifty-meter] depth of water, dune waves begin that are a 328 feet [100 meters] long and scarcely visible to the naked eye, and begin to build up into breakers. Thus one does not flee into shallow water in heavy weather, but into deep water, and one passes sandbanks, if one has the choice, into the lee behind the breaker zone.

Sometimes there are several wave systems simultaneously, with which the sailor has to come to terms. They build up, form cross seas, are influenced by wind and current. Not dangerous, but annoying, is old swell without wind that makes the sail strike.

While wind is invisible, waves build up very impressively. Often we believe we see wind when it is actually the waves that allow us to draw conclusions about the wind. That goes from the first ripples on smooth water, that announce the end of the calm, to the wind-whipped surface of the white foaming sea.

On the one hand, how well a yacht adapts to the waves can be calculated, but the designer's sailing experience also plays a role. The ship should move gently on the crossing of a rough, steep seaway and lose as little way as possible. But it should also move into a glide easily. It should be "stable," show as high, rising moment, but at the same time have a modest, sprinkled surface.

Meeting waves correctly ranks among the most important abilities of helmsmen. In the one-man dinghy the sailor, as living ballast, is the direct antagonist of the wave. On a big yacht under a spinnaker, the helmsman prevents the ship from being thrown off its course by a big wave and "shooting into the sun."

Harro Kniffka with his dragon in a moderate seaway off Sainte-Maxime. Ulli Libor steered the photographer's rubber boat, Prince Alexander of Schleswig-Holstein held Heinrich Hecht firmly during the photographing.

Dinghies at the 2008 Kiel Week. Many dinghy sailors from inland come to the Firth to train for difficult sailing in waves, and to learn about the international competition.

In the Swan World Cup off Sardinia. The timelessly beautiful Swans from Finland have ranked for decades among the seaworthiest yachts on the market.

"One must, to reach the finish line, always sail with the sea, never against it."

Jochen Schümann

New Zealand *while training off San Diego. The Kiwi racer lies perfectly in its own wave. Sailing in the Pacific was familiar to the New Zealanders.*

"The mood on board was electrifying and tumultuous like the sea."

Steven Miller, owner of Mari Cha IV, *about his 2005 Atlantic record.*

Left: The Rubin *off Cowes in 1993. The foreshipman's job is the wettest on board when there are waves, and it costs him strength. – Right: The crew of Corel 45 off Toulon feels good in shorts and T-shirts while the boat glides through the waves, meeting the challenge.*

One man goes forward to set a small foresail. In a classic yacht without a pulpit or rail to catch him, concentration is demanded.

A fight on a crossing. Not a moderate windy sea, but the seaway makes the ships thump.

LIGHT

Seeing with Sharp Eyes

Below: Sunset on the Baltic. Tutima *wins the 260-mile stage from Danzig to Copenhagen in the 2005 Baltic Sprint Cup. – Right: Late afternoon on the way to Fastnet Rock. It promises to be a quiet, maybe even a calm night, for the wind often disappears along with the sun.*

Photographers draw with light, as the name says. Many artists gain a lot of freedom from it and work magic with effects, others consider themselves more as chroniclers of nature. Among the latter is Heinrich Hecht, who sees light and colors everywhere, whereas his writing colleagues put on a show for their nearest conversation partner.

In Hecht's photos, next to nothing is falsified. He uses no filters, he avoids digital "reworking," as major retouching is called today. He chooses the right subjects, has fast cameras, the right film (for the large format), and the best lenses. What Hecht photographs, he has seen in reality. The glowing evening sky, the dinghies in a squall, the dark clouds over the glittering sea. It is good that most of the big events take place before photogenic backgrounds with few clouds. But Hecht also takes pictures in the rain at 3:30 in the morning. The secret of many good photos is that the photographer thinks far ahead and invests effort to have the right light from the right direction at the right place.

When Hecht is on his way as a reporter with a camera, he cannot seek out the best light at the decisive moment. A regatta start is postponed in case of calm or storm, but not because of gray skies or drizzle. When it is real, Hecht is a journalist. But he also sees when a truly fully unspectacular moment—a sailor sitting religiously at the tiller—is made into something special by the light. Or by the lengthening of the light.

The effect of opposing light: Glowing sails in the 2005 Hanseatic-Lloyd Dragon World Championship off Neustadt (right page) and the Dragon Jubilee Regatta of 2004 off Saint-Tropez.

Light not only illuminates our world; it shines through it as well. It makes shadows, it lets sails glow, it lets the atmosphere and the spray glow in the colors of the rainbow. The clear vision after a cold front, the gray water under towering clouds, the blue water on the high sea, an anchorage in the moonlight... We think we see things, but we see light. And one can photograph that. Then one must just recognize which picture composition is worthwhile.

We do not usually realize that we perceive the world for the most part through biological senses. Our brain constantly corrects what our eyes see. A white hull is white for us because we know it is white. It could just as well be orange or blue, depending on what light illuminates it. And even on a gray day, light at sea contains a high UV content. Some broader knowledge about light from everyday life belongs to the photographers and sailors. A polarizing filter in front of a camera lens reduces flare and makes shallow areas or a washed-out horizon emerge clearly. Navigators and helmsmen use Polaroid sunglasses for this reason. And when we take pictures at sea, we should be aware of the composition of light. Otherwise the camera will turn a blue hour into a gray second.

"I, on the other hand, look at the sea with great pleasure dozens of times every day, all the different plays of color that are offered to one in the course of a day."

Pedro Juan Gutierrez

Steer to the north! After a hard regatta day off the Côte d'Azur, it's off to the harbor where the ship is tidied up and there is something warm to eat. Left: It is time for a sundowner. 15 dinghy cruisers on the Steinhuder Meer. The blue-gray wall of clouds as a background makes the spinnakers glow more colorfully in the sun.

Alinghi *at the UBS Trophy off Newport, Rhode Island, on the home waters of the New York Yacht club, in June 2004. At this time of year light winds prevail in this sector of the Atlantic coast. For decades the competitors in the Cup eliminations had the problem of needing a strong-wind ship for the elimination races and then having to meet the defender in a light wind.*

Contrasting subject matter: A bird that flies and a boat that lies, and an evening sky in all the colors of a sunset—but without a sun.

A photo as if by Johann Caspar David Friedrich. The Fastnet fleet passes the Isle of Wight on a western course. The picture gets its panorama from the foreground.

97842

Left page: Champosa *passes the photographer's boat in the opposing light, but the crew has other worries.— Above: The sunlight's reflection makes the wave systems, that the sailing yachts and the unseen motor vessel produce, stand out.*

Boats in the Olympic harbor at Schilksee present themselves to the photographer as if on a silver platter. Thanks to the typical North German rainy weather, one can often see a rainbow over the harbor in the afternoon—but few of us go up in an apartment house to photograph them.

PHIPPS
ALLEN

Black Magic, *as the New Zealanders called their America's Cup challenger in 1995. Hecht photographed the black shark as a fast-moving play of light. – Above: A sunny afternoon in the cockpit releases the same reflexes in the professional photographer as in an amateur: Shoot it!*

A yacht in training for the Timberland Europrix off Cassis. The considerable seaway on the open sea is recognizable by the dark wave troughs in which the boat looks small. The photographer and pilot see the colorful shadow of the sail, but for the crew it does not exist.

Above: Cowes Week, the field of participants in the Channel Race off the Isle of Wight. What begins here in the mild afternoon light is a complex race that makes high demands on crews and navigators. Right: The big one passes the small one, a scissor-picture with the camera.

April weather in June; dark clouds hang over the Schilksee. The cold front has come through, it is clearing up. For tomorrow a sunny sailing day is expected. It was already interesting today.

Palms on the shore, fireworks in the night sky over Valencia. The 32nd America's Cup has brought the seaport on the east coast of Spain into the focal point of the sailing world.

WARNING

Left page: The first lighthouse on the Needles was built on the chalk rock in 1786. Its light at a height of 472 feet [144 meters] could be seen from afar if it did not disappear into deep-hanging clouds. The new lighthouse (of 1859) was thus built at the foot of the cliff and, with five sectors, marks the safe passage to the Solent. – Above: The waters around the Isle of Wight are England's best-known sailing area and significant for sports as well.

Left: The queens of the Nioulargue—the gaff schooner Altair*—on the way into the harbor are always a majestic sight. Their very size impresses. – Above: The foreshipman on the* Cintra*, the oldest surviving classic twelver.*

36

Left page: Defenders' duel: the America's Cup Young America *(behind) and* Stars & Stripes. *To be sure,* Young America *won the elimination races of the defensive candidates, but later she lost, nothing to five, to New Zealand's* Black Magic. – *Below: The star boats of Kiel (Uwe von Below in front) and the spinnaker maneuver on the* Pinta *have a dynamic effect through the glittering brightness that is captured in these photos.*

Left: This yacht, as we know, is white. And the photo reproduces white light correctly, as one can see on the lee rail and right of the mast. But Hecht's picture reveals what light we actually see: the high-frequency blue of the sky, the orange-filtered sun in the Kevlar sail and the water. Above: – A Caribbean dream of all globetrotters: laying at anchor in Admiralty Bay, Bequia.

*Wide, fast, and heavy—*Longobarda *in the Maxi World Cup. With up to a 27-man crew on board, Maxis are the liners of yachting sport. The colorful sail clouds cannot deceive us into thinking that approaching these giants from the bow has little to offer. In this case the photographer's boat is farther away than the telephoto suggests.*

Peter Westphal-Langloh's Formula I racer Becks *on the Firth of Clyde in Scotland, steered by Berend Beilken. Dark skies, strong light, and a pregnant shadow.*

A 34-footer on the west coast of Australia near Fremantle. The "Fremantle Doctor" (or "Doc Freö") is a thermal sea wind that comes up punctually at 2:00 P.M. and stays until the evening hours.

Evening light on board a Corel 45 east of Marseilles. Hecht was on board as the sponsor's photographer. The long exposure time and the prisms of spray on the lens transform the photo at the right into an impressionistic picture.

GER
GER
150

Left page: Europe dinghies on the Steinhuder Meer. Below: The evening atmosphere on the Morning Glory *softens the impression of the momentary photo as soon as a bright flash bathes the ship and crew in white light. At night, the photographer warns the sailors before the flash, so that at least those who are not in the picture can close their eyes. As long as the sun is still above the horizon, this word of caution is not necessary.*

"Earl Grey tea with milk, no sugar"

Samantha Davies before the Vendee Globe Challenge, to the question of what she drinks at sunset.

The air is misty and the barometer falls. The good weather won't last much longer. Europes on the way back from a German championship on the Steinhuder Meer. A summer evening's dream.

Tutima *on the Kiel Firth. Why the crew is trimming is not quite clear. A relic from the afternoon hours when the thermals still supplied wind?*

Heinrich Hecht – Portrait of a Photographer

In search of the ideal picture.

Heinrich Hecht is one of the most requested photographers internationally. His pictures tell of the beauty and might of yachts, their elegance and lightness, the powerful sea, and meditative moments. They tell of the demands of this sport, the accomplishments that people achieve in competition for the best finishes and in battle against the powers of nature. Anyone who sees Hecht's pictures senses that he puts his whole heart into his work. His sailing photos have a recognition value, and what is almost more important, a soul of their own. Where this passion comes from is also understandable from Heinrich Hecht's life story.

Hecht was born in Hannover on August 25, 1955. His family—successful business people from Danzig and passionate sailors. Even his great-grandfather on his mother's side had two small sailing ships, his father had learned shipping merchandising at a shipyard. But when Heinrich grew up, there were no more ships in the family. They had been lost in the war. What the family still retained were great quantities of stories about sailing and a love of the sea. On vacation trips they went to the coast, enjoyed the beach and the water. As homage to this time Heinrich Hecht ventured in 2003 to finance a major project without an employer. For five years he photographed, with his panoramic camera, the German coasts of the North and Baltic Seas. He published the pictures in the unusual 6 x 17 format in two books in 2008.

The work on a coastal project shows a character trait of Heinrich Hecht: When he undertakes something, he sees it through, regardless of all difficulties. Heinrich Hecht then knows no more limits; for him only the right moment for the ideal picture matters.

He had a problematic introduction to photography at the age of three, when he took the already exposed film out of his sister's camera—out of pure curiosity as to what was actually to be seen in the photos. The result: a big sister who was somewhat displeased and a negative film that was black. This experience could not dissuade his interest in photography. His first properly planned pictures with a compact camera were taken on an excursion in Travemünde. Already noticeable then: the child did not concentrate on photographing people standing nearby, but rather still lifes, oldtimers, landscapes—and ships and harbors again and again.

In 1980 a photographer friend advised him to get a "regular" camera. That inspired him to buy his first mirror-reflex camera; it was really a status symbol that raised the owner above the ranks of snapshot-takers. Heinrich Hecht loved photography; it already pleased him, not only to "shoot" pictures but to form them. He photographed by instinct, and that has not changed to this day. But he did not think then of turning his hobby into a profession.

As a young adult he first chose the safe path and built a commercial career in distribution and marketing. He worked for a big computer firm, worked his way up and reached the threshold to a top job in the true sense of the word. With his career near at hand, Hecht had only to sign his contract, but he noticed that he was not really happy. On a slip of paper he had written "photography." He declined the management job.

Photo: Stefano Gattini

Heinrich Hecht is the only photographer who uses the 17 x 6 panoramic camera, a special product with boom number 17, from a helicopter.

It was the turning point in his life. He had decided for the passion instead of the rationale. He took a risk, followed the voice of his heart and fulfilled his dreams. His motto: Some need strength to bear their fate, others use it to build their fate. In 1987 he took some time off. He traveled to London, Los Angeles, and the Fiji Islands, fled there from a typhoon on a 500-meter island, of which the storm left very little, and was on an adventurous trip to the right place at the right time.

At the America's Cup in Fremantle, Australia, Hecht reported for German media when one photo gave him, a blooming beginner in the media business, success that the professionals envied him for: He was the only one to catch, with his lens, the rejoicing Dennis Conner with a champagne bottle; his good luck. Hecht had no accreditation for the victory ceremony and sort of came to victory through the back door. With his camera equipment he climbed over the rubber boats that ring the harbor until he finally stood at the water side of the stage. When Dennis Conner was handed the trophy and champagne, Hecht called, "Dennis!" Conner turned around and Hecht had caught the legendary "Mister America's Cup" from the front as he got the champagne poured over his head. All the others got Conner's champagne shower only from the rear. The photo went around the world and Hecht was suddenly known in one stroke in sailing circles.

Back in Germany, Hecht worked as an editor, reporter, and photographer. His main employer was a radio station. He became the press reporter for the Kiel Week. Two years later, in 1990, he ventured the step into full independence and became a professional photographer.

Then came one spectacular contract after another; Heinrich Hecht now had a reputation. He made exhibits, he photographed the Admiral's Cup, Sardinia Cup, and other great regattas all over the world. He was at the Olympic Games in Barcelona and Sydney, worked on calendars and books, in short, he was in demand. He got to know the sailing scene and interesting people, including Michael Schumacher, Boris Becker, and Queen Silvia of Sweden; a friendship linked him with Prince Felipe of Spain.

Despite his success, Heinrich Hecht did not let up. He belonged to the people who know their roots and know what really true friends are. In 1995 came the highest honor of his profession: he was called to join the official photographic team that was allowed to document the Reichstag's veiling of Jesus. Here Hecht's versatility can be seen, always looking for new themes and motifs. To be sure, sailing is his great passion, but he is also interested in art, architecture, antique cars, and commercial shipping.

In 2000 Heinrich Hecht was constantly at work. He took pictures for the Bertelsmann publishing house at the Expo 2000 in Hannover and traveled to the Olympic Games in Sydney. In the following years he photographed a sales campaign for Timberland, then several calendars for Volkswagen and Land Rover. Working for the Hanseatic Lloyd shipyards, he turned out the photo volume *75 Years of Dragons* and a calendar at Saint-Tropez in 2004. The Dragons were the royalty of the open-keel yachts.

Even though he has sold thousands of pictures, every photo is a new challenge for Heinrich Hecht. There cannot be routine; one is judged anew for every picture—that is one of his maxims. The uneasiness as to whether the results of his jobs are justified—he still feels that before every picture.

In 2006 a new part of life began for Heinrich Hecht. He started a family. Until then only his job mattered, but now Heinrich Hecht became more domesticated. Since then he has enjoyed returning from his business trips to join his wife and daughter in the country near Hannover, where he lives quietly. At the Steinhuder Meer his sailboat awaits him, an H-dinghy from 1959, built of mahogany. For 25 years he has owned it. His goals today: to earn enough money from the work that he likes to do to be able to lead a more carefree life with his family. Professionally he has just one special wish, which he cannot accomplish all by himself: To be present when Germany wins the America's Cup!

Maike Jacobs

Photo: Daniel Forster

The object of desire by regatta sailors all over the world: Heinrich Hecht holding the Holy Grail of the sailing sport, the America's Cup.

Index

ESP
7352
Navantia
IRL
5200
CAM
MUTUAMADRILEÑA
BALEARIA
BALEARIA.com